SO-BBS-223

YOUR LAND AND MY LAND

We Visit

COLOMBIA

Rebecca

Thatcher Murcia

Mitchell Lane

PUBLISHERS
P.O. Box 196
Hockessin, Delaware 19707

Visit
COLOMBIA

YOUR LAND
AND
MY LAND

Brazil

Chile

Colombia

Cuba

Dominican Republic

Mexico

Panama

Peru

Puerto Rico

Venezuela

We Visit

COLOMBIA

Mitchell Lane
PUBLISHERS

Printing   1   2   3   4   5   6   7   8   9

Library of Congress Cataloging-in-Publication Data
Murcia, Rebecca Thatcher, 1962–
  We visit Colombia / by Rebecca Thatcher Murcia.
    p. cm. — (Your land and my land)
  Includes bibliographical references and index.
  ISBN 978-1-58415-885-1 (library bound)
  1. Colombia—Juvenile literature. I. Title.
  F2258.5.M87 2011
  986.1—dc22
                                                          2010026955

PUBLISHER'S NOTE: This story is based on the author's extensive
research, which she believes to be accurate. Documentation of this research
is on page 61.

The Internet sites referenced herein were active as of the publication
date. Due to the fleeting nature of some web sites, we cannot guarantee
they will all be active when you are reading this book.

To reflect current usage, we have chosen to use the secular era
designations BCE ("before the common era") and CE ("of the common
era") instead of the traditional designations BC ("before Christ") and AD
(*anno Domini,* "in the year of the Lord").

PLB

Contents

Introduction

Latin America is known for vibrant mixtures of cultures and cuisines, for tropical paradises and colorful wildlife, and in some places, for violent weather and political turmoil. *Latin America* is the name given to the regions of North, Central, and South America where languages based on Latin are spoken. Those languages include Spanish, Portuguese, and some variations of French.

People in the United States commonly think of all nations south of the U.S. border as being part of Latin America. It includes Mexico, many of the Caribbean Islands, and the countries in Central America and South America. Colombia is in the northernmost part of South America. From the craggy Andean peaks to the beaches on the Caribbean Sea, Colombia is full of variety and contrasts.

The Regions and Countries of Latin America

LATIN AMERICA

Caribbean: Cuba, the Dominican Republic, French West Indies, Haiti, and Puerto Rico (U.S.)
North America: Mexico
Central America: Belize, Costa Rica, El Salvador, Guatemala, Honduras, Nicaragua, Panama
South America: Argentina, Bolivia, Brazil, Chile, Colombia, Ecuador, French Guiana, Guyana, Paraguay, Peru, Suriname, Uruguay, Venezuela

All the fighting does not negate what is good about Colombia. It is a country of wonderous geography, from the vast eastern plains that are important environmentally to the towering Andes whose ancient volcanoes contribute to the richness of the Andean soil. Colombia's history, like its geography, is full of contradictions. It is sometimes considered the country with the longest history of democracy in Latin America. But it is also the country with the longest civil war in Latin America.

Colombia's cultural traditions are very rich. European settlers brought their accordions. Africans brought their drums and rhythms. The musical traditions blended to form what has become Colombia's internationally famous vallenato folk music. Carlos Vives and Juanes—in addition to Shakira—are Colombian singers who have become known around the world.

Colombians are famous not just for their music. Gabriel Gárcia Márquez became a kind of spokesman for the difficulties—and magic—of Latin America when he penned *One Hundred Years of Solitude*, which rose to be an emblematic work on small-town Latin America. In 1982 he won the Nobel Prize for literature with praise for "his novels and short stories, in which the fantastic and the realistic are combined in a richly-composed world of imagination reflecting a continent's life and conflicts."[1]

The government of Colombia has been promoting tourism to the country with the slogan, "The only danger is that you are going to want to stay."[2] While that slogan is not entirely true, it highlights Colombia's uniqueness and beauty. Welcome to Colombia.

Chía, Cundinamarca, Andes Mountains, Sabana de Bogotá

WHERE IN THE WORLD IS COLOMBIA?

Where in the World

Caribbean
Sea

NETHERLANDS ANTILLES
(Netherlands)

Willemstad

Certain islands of the
Archipiélago de San Andrés
y Providencia (13°00'N,
81°30'W) and the Isla de
Malpelo 3°58'N, 81°35'W)
belonging to Colombia are
not shown on this map.

Santa
Marta
Ríohacha
LA
GUAJIRA

Barranquilla
ATLÁNTICO
Ciénaga
Cartagena
Valledupar
Maracaibo
Lago de
Maracaibo
Valencia
La G
Cara

MAGDALENA
CESAR

Tolú
Sincelejo
Montería
SUCRE
NORTE
DE
SANTANDER
VENEZUELA

Turbo
CÓRDOBA
BOLÍVAR
Cúcuta
Pamplona

PANAMA
Panama

Bucaramanga
Arauca
Puerto
Carreño
ANTIOQUIA
SANTANDER
ARAUCA

North
Pacific
Ocean

Medellín
Barbosa
Paz de Río
CASANARE
VICHADA

Quibdó
BOYACÁ
Tunja
Yopal

CHOCÓ
CALDAS
Manizales
RISARALDA
Pereira
CUNDINAMARCA
Bogotá
Puerto López
Puerto
Inírida

Armenia
Ibagué
Girardot
QUINDÍO
Villavicencio
DISTRITO
ESPECIAL

Buenaventura
VALLE
DEL
CAUCA
TOLIMA
META
GUAINÍA

Cali
Neiva
San José del
Guaviare
Río Guainía

CAUCA
HUILA
Mitú

Popayán
GUAVIARE
VAUPÉS

Tumaco
NARIÑO
Florencia

Pasto
Mocoa
CAQUETÁ
BRAZIL

Ipiales
PUTAMAYO

Quito

ECUADOR
AMAZONAS

Colombia

—————— International boundary
—·—·—·— Internal administrative
         boundary
★   National capital
◉   Internal administrative
         capital
+++++++ Railroad
—————— Road

PERU

| 0 | 50 | 100 | 150 Kilometers |
| 0 | 50 | 100 | 150 Miles |

Iquitos
Leticia

Boundary representation
not necessarily authoritat

COLOMBIAN FACTS AT A GLANCE

Official name: Republic of Colombia

Capital: Bogotá

Size: 707,688 square miles (1,138,914 square kilometers)—almost twice the size of Texas

Land area: 689,165 square miles (1,109,104 square kilometers)

Water area: 62,268 square miles (100,210 square kilometers)

Cattleya trianae orchid

Highest point: Pico Cristóbal Colón—18,947 feet (5,775 meters)

Lowest point: Pacific Ocean—0 feet (0 meters)

Population: 44,205,293 (2010 estimate)

Ethnic groups: mestizo 58%, white 20%, mulatto 14%, black 4%, mixed black-Amerindian 3%, Amerindian 1%

Official language: Spanish

Exports: petroleum, coffee, coal, nickel, emeralds, apparel, bananas, cut flowers

Imports: industrial equipment, transportation equipment, consumer goods, chemicals, paper products, fuels, electricity

Crops: coffee, cut flowers, bananas, rice, tobacco, corn, sugarcane, cocoa beans, oilseed, vegetables; forest products; shrimp

Flag: The Colombian flag retains the three main colors of the banner of Gran Colombia, the short-lived republic that broke up in 1830. Various interpretations of the colors exist, including yellow for the gold in Colombia's land, blue for the seas on its shores, and red for the blood spilled for freedom. The colors have also been described as representing sovereignty and justice (yellow), loyalty and vigilance (blue), and bravery and generosity (red); or simply liberty, equality, and fraternity.

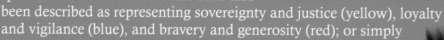

National flower: *Cattleya trianae* orchid

National bird: Andean condor

Source: *CIA World Factbook*, Colombia

Archaeologists are still investigating the pre-Columbian statues found in an area around San Augustín in the state of Huila. Although little is known about the ancient artists, efforts are under way to find out more about the statues and how they can be used to develop tourism.

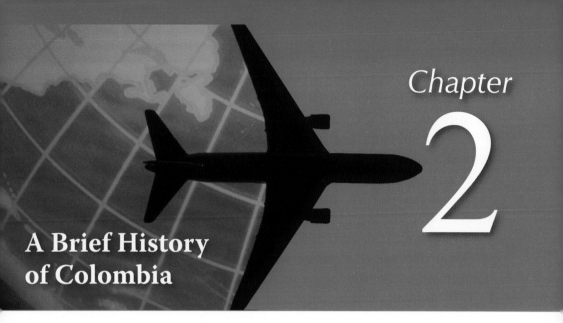

A Brief History of Colombia

Although Colombia is named after Christopher Columbus, the famous explorer never actually arrived in what is now Colombia. Gonzalo Jiménez de Quesada, a Spanish lawyer, led an expedition into the interior of what was then known as New Granada in 1536. The force ran out of food and lost hundreds of men to hunger and tropical illnesses, but when they eventually arrived in what became Bogotá, Colombia's capital, they found the natives growing potatoes, which were unknown in Europe. Explorers brought the potato back to Europe, where it was replanted and soon became a staple of the European diet.

There were many different tribes of native people living in Colombia at the time of the conquest. Although Colombia does not have any extraordinary ruins like those of the Incas of Peru or the Maya of Mexico, the indigenous people did create intricate and fascinating works with gold, rock, and weaving. Little is known about the native people who created a mysterious complex of sculptures and burial sites throughout an area known as San Augustín, but archaeologists are continuing to study the area and unearth statues and gravesites.

The encounter with the early explorers did not bode well for the native people of Colombia. Many were killed or forced into slavery. They also succumbed to smallpox because they had no immunity to the disease when it arrived from Europe. However, many native people survived by making peace with the colonists, and today Colombia still has small indigenous populations scattered throughout the country.

Colonists brought people from Africa to work as slaves and formed large plantations for growing sugar, bananas, and other crops. They also began digging huge mines in order to remove Colombia's many minerals, such as gold and emeralds. Salt was mined from the mountains around Zipaquirá, near what is now Bogotá. The one-time salt mine was later turned into a huge underground cathedral that tourists from around the world enjoy visiting.

After about 200 years of Spanish colonial rule—and amidst disarray in Spain because of fighting with France's Napoleon—the elites of Colombia and the rest of Latin America began clamoring for self-rule in 1810. Instead of organizing into a united revolutionary organization, leaders in different parts of the country declared independence on their own. They also fought among themselves, depending on whether they wanted a conservative, centrist government or a federalist system. Colombian historians have since dubbed this era the time of the "Foolish Fatherland." Spain fought back against the push for independence, but the colonists, eventually led by Simón Bolívar, won independence in 1819. Bolívar dreamed of a "Gran Colombia," a nation that would encompass what would later be Venezuela, Colombia, Panama, and Ecuador in one large, powerful country. It was not to be.

Bolívar at one point named himself dictator of the whole region in an attempt to keep the areas united as Gran Colombia, but by 1830 the union was dissolved into smaller countries. Bolívar's influence continued, as he formed what would become a powerful force in Colombia's future: the Conservative Party. This group believed in a centralized, powerful government and a close alliance with the Catholic Church. Leaders opposed to the Conservative Party's ideas formed the Liberal Party, which believed in a more populist and democratic structure for Colombia's government.

The two parties exchanged power in Colombia throughout the late 1800s and 1900s, sometimes peacefully and sometimes violently. One of the worst wars between the two parties was what became known as the War of a Thousand Days, from 1899 to 1902. While Colombian leaders were focused on the fighting between the two parties, the United States, which wanted to build a canal across the Central American isthmus, promoted the secession of Panama from Colombia. After

The Bolivar Monument near the Boyaca Bridge in Colombia commemorates the 1819 victory over the Spanish Army.

the Colombian Senate refused to grant Panama's independence, U.S. troops landed in Panama in 1903 and declared it a sovereign nation.

Around that time, in 1898, Jorge Eliécer Gaitán was born in a small town near Bogotá. When Gaitán was a politically active young man and lawyer, banana workers in the north of Colombia went on strike. The workers demanded an eight-hour day and other concessions from their employer, the large American United Fruit Company. Tensions grew in the banana zone, and the Colombian government sent soldiers. Initially the soldiers killed 13 workers, and then about 60 more.[1]

Gaitán investigated the massacre of the banana workers and demanded justice. He became an important Liberal Party leader. In 1948, he campaigned for president, gathering huge crowds with powerful speeches that denounced the rich people of Colombia. He was assassinated on April 9, 1948, while walking to a restaurant in Bogotá. In response to the assassination, violence broke out across the city. It spread throughout Colombia, with Conservatives killing Liberals and Liberals killing Conservatives for the next ten years in what became known as La Violencia, or The Violence.

In 1953, the military took over the government and installed General Gustavo Rojas as president. Rojas became a popular leader as he sought to curb the violence, and his daughter organized new social programs for the benefit of the nation's poor. In 1958, Conservative and Liberal leaders decided to take turns at the presidency. Although this arrangement contributed to peace between the parties, it led to the formation of guerrilla groups who felt excluded from the political process. Pedro Antonio Marín, who also was known as Manuel Marulanda and "Tirofijo," or "Sureshot," founded the FARC, which would become the dominant guerrilla group in Colombia.

During the 1960s and 1970s, the market for cocaine grew exponentially. At first the FARC only taxed the drug traffickers, but later it became more directly involved in drug trafficking. To defend themselves from the FARC and other groups, landowners started armies known as paramilitaries. These also became involved in drug trafficking.

FYI FACT: The M-19 guerrilla movement was founded soon after April 19, 1970, when a popular conservative general, Gustavo Rojas, lost an election, and many of his supporters thought fraud was involved. The M-19 became famous—and somewhat popular—after they committed several audacious acts before laying down their arms and becoming a political party in the late 1980s. They stole Simón Bolívar's sword from a museum and took the entire embassy of the Dominican Republic hostage in 1980.

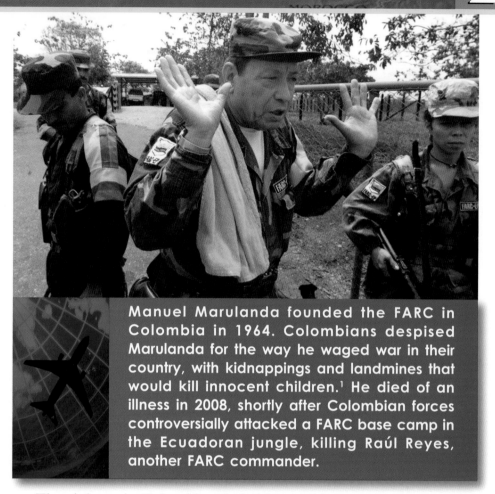

Manuel Marulanda founded the FARC in Colombia in 1964. Colombians despised Marulanda for the way he waged war in their country, with kidnappings and landmines that would kill innocent children.[1] He died of an illness in 2008, shortly after Colombian forces controversially attacked a FARC base camp in the Ecuadoran jungle, killing Raúl Reyes, another FARC commander.

The violence in Colombia—fueled by wealth from the international drug trade—grew worse in the 1990s, when Ernesto Samper was elected with the help of drug money. Andrés Pastrana, the next president, surrendered a large area of southern Colombia to the FARC, hoping to jumpstart the peace process, but the FARC only used the zone to expand their drug trafficking and kidnapping.

Alvaro Uribe, whose father was killed by guerrillas, was elected president in 2002 and re-elected in 2006. Although people continued to admire him for his hard work and dedication to bringing peace to Colombia, human rights advocates have claimed his government has indiscriminately killed innocent civilians in the battle against the guerrillas. Uribe's defense minister, Juan Manuel Santos, was elected to succeed him in 2010.

Nevado del Ruiz is one of Colombia's several high, snow-capped mountain peaks. Hikers who are in good physical shape enjoy walking and climbing up the mountains, but they must take precautions because the air is extremely thin at such high altitudes.

From the snow-capped peaks of the Andes to the Amazonian riverbeds, Colombia's terrain, flora, and fauna are truly incredible. Colombia has an extensive system of national parks and nature preserves that seek to protect the country's extreme biodiversity, but unfortunately the system is not enough. Deforestation, development, drug trafficking, and spraying herbicides to counter drug trafficking are all taking their toll on Colombia's environment, and some of Colombia's famous rare species—such as the South American mahogany tree and the Andean condor—are endangered.

Starting in the north, the San Andrés Archipelago is an extraordinary collection of islands in the Caribbean. They are home to coral reefs, mangroves, and a sea flower biosphere preserve that has been recognized by the United Nations.

The mountains of Santa Marta, on Colombia's Caribbean coast, include Pico Cristóbal Colón, which is the highest peak in Colombia and the tallest coastal mountain in the world. One of the indigenous tribes of Santa Marta calls itself the "Elder Brothers" of humanity. The tribe, known as the Kogi, believes that it is the oldest human community on earth, and that it has a responsibility to warn the rest of the humans that mining and other industries are destroying the planet.

At the foot of the mountain, the Parque Tayrona nature preserve also includes stunning views, coral reefs, and beautiful beaches. To the east along the coast lies the large Guajira Desert, which is the driest part of Colombia. To the south and west lies the Chocó, an area near the Panamanian border which is one of the rainiest parts of the country.

The Magdalena River, which is similar to the U.S. Mississippi, is a huge, beautiful river that courses from the Andean highlands to the Caribbean. It could be an environmental jewel, but it is heavily polluted.

The Andes Mountains, which begin in Chile in the southern tip of South America and continue all the way to Colombia, are one of the most important aspects of Colombian geography. Divided into three ranges in Colombia, they provide a wide variety of climates and growing conditions for crops, from the cold higher elevations to the warmer valleys. The Andean region is host to the endangered spectacled bear, the only bear in South America; the endangered Andean condor; and a record number of elegant orchids, unusual flowers that grow on trees or rocks, often without soil.

The central range of the Andes has several volcanoes, most notably the Nevado del Ruiz, which erupted in 1985. A flow of lava and mud, known as lahar, traveled to the town of Armero and killed almost the entire town as they slept. Another volcano near the southern city of Pasto, Galeras, has been mostly dormant. When it erupted in 1993, it killed six scientists who had gathered in the city for a conference on volcanoes.[1]

The coffee-growing land that lies across the Central Ranges of the Colombian Andes is probably one of the most emblematic of Colombia. Many Americans are familiar with images of Colombian coffee growers' iconic representative, Juan Valdez, as he harvests coffee on the slopes of a typical coffee farm. Colombia has long been a center for coffee growing because coffee bushes grow better at higher altitudes.

The World Wildlife Fund named the Llanos of Colombia, or the Plains, as one of the 200 most important eco-regions in the world. The Llanos, which extend east from the Andes toward the border with Venezuela, have long been known as a somewhat barren area, only capable of offering forage for cattle and subterranean oil. However, the Llanos support animals such as the caiman, the anaconda, and perhaps

Capybaras eat mainly grasses and aquatic plants. They live near water, and when they dive, they can stay under for up to five minutes. Their name means "master of the grasses" in the language of the Guaranis, a major South American indigenous group.

most notably, the capybara, a rodent that is as big as a medium-sized dog. Catholic priests once ruled that the capybara was a fish, and thus acceptable to eat on Fridays. This could have led to the capybara's extermination, but the species is still numerous in many parts of Colombia.

Finally, the Amazon region of Colombia is host to hundreds of unusual species such as the sloth, the white-faced capuchin monkey, the giant anteater, and the jaguar. The Colombian Amazon, like the Amazon area of Brazil and Peru, is known as the lungs of the world because its trees produce so much oxygen.

FYI FACT:

Colombia also governs Isla de Malpelo, or Bad Hair Island, about 235 miles (380 kilometers) off the Pacific Coast. The sea around the island is home to rare sharks, and fishing is off-limits there.

Las Lajas, a large cathedral that was built in a river canyon near the town of Ipiales in southern Colombia, underscores the importance of the Catholic Church in Colombia. Although Protestant churches have become more popular in recent years, the Catholic Church remains a very popular and powerful institution throughout the country.

Chapter 4

The People

Colombia is a racially diverse country. In colonial times, new Colombians were born of relationships between Europeans and native peoples. Afro-Colombians, who trace their ancestry to slaves brought to Colombia after the conquest, make up about 10 percent of the Colombian population. Like the United States, Colombia also has immigrants from around the world. Colombian singer Shakira's father, for example, was originally from Lebanon.

Colombia's citizens are overwhelmingly Catholic. Although the Catholic Church is no longer the hugely powerful influence it once was, most Colombians still consider themselves Catholic and want their children to be baptized in the Catholic Church. First communion is also seen as an important ritual. Even parents with very little money will somehow find a way to buy their son or daughter an extravagant outfit and host a large party to celebrate their child's first communion.

As the Catholic Church's power wanes, Protestant churches, known as "evangelicals" in Colombia, are growing in size and popularity. Many of the large Protestant denominations in the United States, such as the Presbyterians, the Mennonites, and the Lutherans, have churches in Colombia. Although their numbers are small, Muslims and Jews also practice there. Small populations of native people continue to practice their traditional faiths.

The Catholic Church's calendar, however, continues to dominate the official schedule of holidays. In order to promote leisure activities and family time, most holidays are celebrated on Mondays so that workers have a three-day weekend. Holy week, between Palm Sunday and Easter, is a required vacation from school. Other holidays are the same as those in the United States, such as Christmas and New Year's. Colombian Independence Day is July 20. The International Day of the Woman, March 8, is often marked in schools with singing and dancing.

Education in Colombia is widely varied, but one thing remains true at any school in Colombia, from the most humble preschool to the most prestigious high schools: all require uniforms. In addition to a more formal uniform, students usually have a sweat suit–type outfit for physical education days. Because of the years of violence, there

In a school in Bogotá, children wear smocks over their uniforms during art class. Some schools require students to wear ties, but uniforms are usually white, button-down shirts or polo shirts with slacks or skirts.

Indigenous people have been especially victimized by the violence in the countryside. When they flee to the cities, they often have trouble finding places to live, work, and worship.

are areas of the country where there are no police, health care clinics, or schools. Some rural areas have only elementary schools. Other parts of the country have better public education, but the public schools tend to be overcrowded and underfunded. On the other hand, Colombia's private schools and universities rival private schools and universities anywhere in the world. The public National University, whose main campus is in Bogotá, is also highly regarded throughout Latin America.

Although Colombian people tend to have large, close-knit extended families, Colombians have become travelers, largely because of the poverty and violence in their country. More than 3 million Colombians have been forced to leave their homes and move to cities or to other countries such as the United States, Venezuela, Ecuador, or Spain. Many of them wind up in shantytowns surrounding the bigger cities. The United Nations and many international aid groups are working with the Colombian government to help the war refugees.

A teenage boy enjoys a game of street soccer in the afternoon sun in La Mesa, Cundinamarca. Neighborhoods throughout Colombia have street soccer courts that are also suitable for volleyball and basketball. Soccer is by far the most popular sport.

Culture and Lifestyle

Despite the problems with poverty, violence, and war in their country, Colombians are a surprisingly happy people. In fact, in a 2006 Gallup poll, Colombians scored the highest for happiness in the world.[1]

One reason for this may be that Colombians know how to play. It could almost be said that wherever there are two Colombians, they are playing a game of *something*.

Colombians are passionate about basketball, bicycle racing, tennis, weightlifting, judo—even Ping-Pong (table tennis), but soccer is their most popular sport. Colombians play soccer on paved basketball courts that dot most neighborhoods, on streets and sidewalks, at school, and in vacant lots, pastures, and stadiums all over the country. Every Colombian city has at least one professional soccer team, and Bogotá has three. Sometimes Colombians' passion for soccer can get out of control. Soccer hooliganism, which has been a problem for years in Europe, also occurs in Colombia. Andrés Escobar, a member of Colombia's national soccer team, was murdered shortly after the 1994 World Cup. Escobar's killer was upset because Escobar had scored a goal against Colombia—known as an "own goal"—at the World Cup.

Colombia does not have big racecar tracks like those used in NASCAR or Formula One, so car races are held on winding roads in the mountains. Juan Pablo Montoya, a Colombian racecar driver, started his career driving in Colombian kart races.

Tejo, which is like a cross between bowling and darts, is a very popular game Colombians inherited from their indigenous ancestors.

Players throw a heavy metal disk at a target. The target holds small fuses that will explode if they are hit hard enough.

Besides sports, Colombians also enjoy hiking, horseback riding, dancing, and other forms of exercise. Although the civil war once prevented Colombians from enjoying some of their country's natural beauty, that has changed in recent years. Families and groups of people travel throughout the country to hike to the snow line of Nevado del Ruiz, for example, or to enjoy the country's beaches.

Chess is also played throughout Colombia. Chess players often enjoy the game outside in city parks and other gathering places. Colombian newspapers often have stories about international chess matches in their sports sections.

In Cartagena, the Teatro Colon and the Teatro Cartagena are severely deteriorated. Theater fans in Colombia hope to upgrade the theaters and begin using them again.

Colombians love drama, whether it is at the movies, live in theaters, or on television. Bogotá hosts one of the biggest theater festivals in the world every year; many cities have at least one theater company. Movies are very popular. A small Colombian film industry competes only faintly with movies that are brought in from Hollywood, often very soon after their release dates in the United States.

And finally, Colombians, just like people everywhere, love their television sets, especially their telenovelas, or soap operas. A Colombian soap opera called *Ugly Betty* was so successful that an American version was created starring America Ferrera.

Colombian coffee growers have had great success promoting their coffee as the best in the world. Colombians tend to drink their coffee black, in small mugs, during several coffee breaks during the day. They often sweeten it with raw sugar, known in Colombia as *panela*.

Economy and Commerce

The Colombian economy has many strengths. The country has abundant natural resources, a hardworking population, and a high level of education. Unfortunately its economy is often hampered by the danger and insecurity that have been present throughout its recent history. The development of roads and highways, while proceeding steadily, has also been slowed by the difficult terrain in the Andes mountains. There are concerns that some of the economic activity, such as mining and the excessive cultivation of flowers in greenhouses, is damaging the country's unique environment. Nevertheless, Colombia's economy continues to grow.

Oil is one of the engines in Colombia's economy. Ecopetrol, the state-owned oil company, recently sold shares to the public for the first time and is one of Colombia's largest employers. ExxonMobil and several smaller oil companies are also prominent in the Colombian oil market.

Colombians love their cars. Both General Motors (GM) and Renault, a French company, have been manufacturing cars in Colombia for many years. Colmotores, which is a branch of GM, manufactures and sells many cars, trucks, and buses in Colombia.

Agricultural exports of coffee and bananas are another backbone of Colombia's economy. In addition, Colombians have been growing more and more flowers for export to the United States. The flower trade, however, is becoming increasingly controversial as human rights experts and environmentalists say workers and the environment are being exposed to too many chemicals in an effort to grow flowers that will look perfect when they are unloaded in the United States.

Within Colombia, the national chocolate industry has thrived. Small farmers also grow and process raw sugar, which is still the sweetener of choice in many Colombian homes. There are also parts of Colombia, such as the Magdalena Valley and the eastern plains, where cattle ranching is big business.

The Internet and cellular phones have become extremely popular in recent years. All across the country, people have started businesses selling calls on cell phones and minutes on the Internet. Because of the difficulty of establishing telephone lines (thieves find the copper profitable and easy to take down), high-speed Internet has been slow to spread across the country. Colombian engineers have found creative solutions, including broadcasting Internet signals through the air.

For more than 50 years, all major Colombian companies and government agencies have been required to give four percent of each worker's salary to a family benefit fund. Some of these family benefit funds have become big businesses. Colsubsidio, for example, is now a major employer in Colombia. It owns supermarkets, hotels, clinics, and a large and popular amusement park called Piscilago. Another family benefit fund, Compensar, has focused more on sports and sponsors a professional soccer team.

These family benefit funds, however, do little for the families that earn too little to belong. Extreme inequality—with a few Colombians

Piscilago

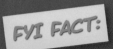
among the richest people in the world and the majority just barely surviving—remains a problem in Colombia.

Although Colombian officials don't like to admit it, profits from drug trafficking also fuel the Colombian economy. Drug money goes into hotels, restaurants, houses, cars, and shopping malls. Drug traffickers employ farmworkers who strip the coca leaves off the bushes, chemists who turn the leaves into cocaine, accountants who handle the finances, and lawyers who represent them in court. Colombian drug traffickers also produce heroin. The vast majority of the drugs produced in Colombia are exported to the United States and other countries, where the high prices drug users and addicts pay contributes to the ongoing violence in Colombia.

Juan Manuel Santos, whose family has a long tradition in politics and newspapers, grew up in Bogotá. He earned advanced degrees from colleges in Kansas, London, and Massachusetts. As defense minister under Álvaro Uribe, Santos made several successful strikes against the FARC and headed the 2002 rescue of Ingrid Betancourt and fourteen other hostages. He was elected president of Colombia in June 2010.

Politics and Government

In Colombia, the democracy starts at the lowest level. Every neighborhood has a communal action committee with a president and other officers. These committees are in charge of organizing neighborhood-level activities, such as sports teams, and handling any problems that might occur with utilities such as water. Each city has a mayor who is responsible for serving the local population's needs in matters such as trash removal, road repair, and regulating development.

Departments are similar to states in the United States. Colombia has 32 departments as well as Bogotá, the capital city. Each department has a governor and an assembly responsible for managing the area's schools, roads, and other areas such as health.

On the national level, Colombia has three branches of government similar to the United States. There is the executive branch, with a president and a vice president, the judicial branch, the Supreme Court and lower courts, and the legislative branch. The legislature includes the Senate, which has 100 senators elected from districts throughout the country and two senators representing the indigenous people of Colombia. The House of Representatives has 166 members representing districts, plus two who represent indigenous Colombians, one who represents Colombians who live in other countries, and one who represents political minorities.

The Colombian Constitution, which was rewritten in 1991 to make the country more democratic, prohibits presidents from serving for more than two terms.

FYI FACT:

The Colombian military, which is part of the executive branch, organized a daring rescue of fifteen hostages, including three U.S. military contractors, in 2008. The military tricked the FARC guerrillas into giving up the hostages in what was later chronicled in an American bestseller called *Out of Captivity: Surviving 1,967 Days in the Colombian Jungle.*[1]

OUT of CAPTIVITY
Surviving 1,967 Days in the Colombian Jungle

MARC GONSALVES, KEITH STANSELL, AND TOM HOWES WITH GARY BROZEK

Presidential Palace
Casa de Nariño in
Bogotá, Colombia

Ingrid Betancourt was a popular senator when she was kidnapped during a presidential campaign in 2002. In 2010, two years after she was freed, she damaged her reputation by threatening to sue the government for $6.8 million. She withdrew the demand but was widely criticized for filing it in the first place.

Famous People

Famous Colombians include writers, singers, athletes, and other artists. Some of the Colombians who are included in this chapter no longer live in Colombia full time, but they all continue to love their home country and hope that one day Colombia will truly be at peace.

Ingrid Betancourt

Ingrid Betancourt was born in Bogotá in 1961 and grew up as a child of privilege. Her father was a diplomat who worked for the United Nations. Her mother was a beauty queen who was also passionate about helping the poor of Colombia.

Betancourt studied in France while her father worked for the United Nations. Her parents always kept her informed of what was going on in Colombia, and as a young woman she returned to Colombia and began working for change. She opposed the rampant corruption in the government and pushed for better treatment of Colombia's environment.

She was elected to the Senate in 1998. In 2002 she decided to run for president of Colombia. Betancourt and her campaign manager, Clara Rojas, ventured into guerrilla territory and were captured by the FARC.

Betancourt was held until 2008, when the Colombian military rescued her by tricking the FARC into handing over her and fourteen other hostages. Since the rescue, she has been living in France and working on a book about her ordeal as a hostage.

Fernando Botero

Fernando Botero, whose signature oversized people and animals decorate parks, museums, and private collections, is easily Colombia's most famous visual artist.

Botero was born in Medellín in 1932 and began his artistic career as a boy who drew bullfighters and bulls in his notebooks. He became fascinated with painting as a young man and was kicked out of one high school because of the radical ideas he espoused in a newspaper article he wrote titled "Picasso and Non-Conformity in Art."

Botero first became internationally famous in 1961 when New York City's Museum of Modern Art bought his painting of a plump young Mona Lisa. Over the next few decades he gradually became known as a master painter and sculptor.

In 2005, he was distraught over allegations of torture in an American-run jail, Abu Ghraib, in Iraq. He created an entire show of paintings and drawings depicting the treatment of prisoners. The exhibit, entitled Abu Ghraib, was praised for sharing Botero's outrage about what had happened at the prison.[1]

Gabriel García Márquez

Gabriel García Márquez was born in Aracataca, a small town in Colombia's northern banana-growing region, in 1927. He has often said that he became such a good writer because while he was growing up his grandmother told him fantastic ghost stories and his grandfather told him true stories of Colombia's violent history.

García Márquez planned on becoming a lawyer, and studied law at the National University in Bogotá. While there, his rooming house was burned down in the violence that followed the assassination of

presidential candidate Jorge Eliéc-er Gaitán. The young student, who had already demonstrated a talent for writing, transferred to the University of Cartagena and began writing articles for the newspaper there.

He belonged to a writers' group and began working on his first novel, *Leaf Storm,* which had limited success. His second novel, *One Hundred Years of Solitude,* was about a rural family in a fictional Latin American town. The in-trigue, the bizarre happenings, and the beautiful writing made the book a huge hit. García Márquez won the Nobel Prize for literature in 1982 and went on to write other great novels, such as *Love in the Time of Cholera* and *The General in His Labyrinth.*

Shakira

Shakira Isabel Mebarak Ripoll was born in 1977 in Barranquilla, a large city on the Colombian coast. Her father was originally from Lebanon. As a young child she showed a surprising singing talent and naturally learned how to belly dance.

Shakira's parents recognized their daughter's potential and en-rolled her in classes to learn acting, dancing, and singing. Shakira and her mother moved to Bogotá, and Shakira starred in a television soap opera. Her first priority was always writing songs and singing.

Her first two albums met with only modest success, but she kept writing songs and looking for the best possible producers and musicians to help her. When she was nineteen, she produced *Pies Descalzos* (Bare Feet). The album became a national and international phenomenon, and it launched her into a highly successful career. Since then, she has had many other hit recordings. She performed "Hips Don't Lie" with Wyclef Jean at the 2006 soccer World Cup final and "Waka Waka" at the 2010 final.

Shakira has also become deeply involved in philanthropy. Her foundation has built five schools in Colombia, and she has worked hard to persuade Latin American governments to invest in early childhood education.

Carlos Valderrama

Carlos Valderrama was once one of the most recognizable soccer players in the world. When he played for Colombia during the 1990, 1994, and 1998 World Cups, he became well known for his perfect passes and his bright blond afro.

Valderrama was born in 1961 in Santa Marta. His father was a professional soccer player. As a child, Valderrama learned to play soccer at school and in neighborhood games. He started playing professionally for Union Magdalena when he was twenty years old, and went on to play for other Colombian and European teams before joining Major League Soccer (MLS) in 1996. He played for the Miami Fusion, the Tampa Bay Mutiny, and the Colorado Rapids in the United States. Although he came to MLS toward the end of his career as a professional soccer player, Valderrama recorded an impressive 114 assists (passes that led to goals), which put him in second place in the history of the league.[2]

In 2004 he held a retirement game with many of his soccer-playing friends and the Colombian singer Carlos Vives. The stadium was packed with 59,000 fans. He has since starred in a reality TV show and worked as a soccer coach and an ambassador for MLS.

Jaime Garzón

Jaime Garzón was a Colombian comedian and journalist who made fun of Colombia's leaders and politicians. One of his favorite characters was a boy who interviewed Colombia's leaders while he shined their shoes.

In the 1990s, Garzón worked as a mediator between guerrilla groups and the government, and helped co-ordinate the release of hostages. A paramilitary leader accused him of being a guerrilla supporter and or-dered him killed. Garzón was shot on August 13, 1999, on the way to his job at a radio station.

The huge outpouring of mourners at his outdoor funeral showed how much Colombians loved Garzón's work—both as a humorist and as a humanitarian.

Carlos Castañeda, a Colombian coffee grower, became the new Juan Valdez in 2006. In the role of Juan Valdez, Castañeda travels to the Medellín Flower Festival and other events around the world to promote Colombia's coffee.

Festivals and Attractions

Any discussion of Colombia's festivals must begin with Carnival in Barranquilla. Although it is not as famous as the carnivals of New Orleans or Rio de Janeiro, the Carnival of Barranquilla is spectacular in its own right.

For four days before Ash Wednesday, which signals the beginning of the Lenten period prior to Easter, people from across Colombia converge in Barranquilla for concerts, parades, festivals, comedic theater, and a beauty pageant. Carnival celebrates the mix of cultures that make up Colombia, especially on the coast, where the African influence remains strong in the music and the dance. Barranquilla's Carnival is so outstanding that the United Nations Educational, Cultural and Scientific Organization recognized it as an important cultural event that needs to be protected.

Continuing up the coast from Barranquilla, another famous festival is held every

Barranquilla Carnival

year in April. It's the Vallenato Legends Festival and it attracts fans of vallenato, an accordion-based Colombian folk music, from throughout Colombia and the world. The festival features contests for accordion players and other musicians.

The department known as the Guajira is the northern-most part of South America. It is home to El Cerrejon, the largest open-pit coal mine in the world. It is also very dry, with areas of desert. Members of the Wayuu indigenous group from both Venezuela and Colombia gather in the Guajira town of Uribia in early summer for two days of parades, concerts, horse races, and games that have been played by the indig-enous people for centuries. There are also sales and exhibitions of traditional Wayuu crafts, such as weaving, ceramics, and containers made out of the calabash, a gourd-like fruit that grows on trees in Colombia.

Like many of the holidays on the Colombian calendar, the an-nual festival in Anolaima is a Catholic festival. The Corpus Christi festival in Anolaima, near Bogotá, is based on a celebration of the Eucharist, a ritual in which Catholics take communion by sym-bolically eating bread that represents Christ's body and drinking wine that represents his blood. It is held near the end of June. Anolaima is a picturesque town that is known as the fruit capital of Colombia. Farmers parade through the streets carrying elaborate arches decorated with fruit. The local bishop holds masses, and the holy sacraments are paraded throughout the town. There are also contests to choose the most beautiful fruit and the obligatory beauty pageant.

The Bogotá International Book Fair attracts readers and students from throughout the capital area. Every year the festival invites writers and editors from other countries to be featured guests of the festival, which includes lectures, readings, discussions, and lots of book sales.

Medellín is the second largest city in Colombia. After suffering from terrible drug-related violence in the 1990s, Medellín has emerged as a modern, progressive city that hosts many different types of meetings, sports events, conferences, and festivals throughout the year. Two that are particularly important are the flower festival and the bullfighting festival.

The flower festival features artisans who carry elaborate flower arrangements in parades. The flower festival has hosted huge horse and car parades as well.

The bullfighting festival goes on for about a month over August and September. Bullfighting in La Macarena, Medellín's new state-of-the-art bullfighting stadium with a retractable roof, is the focus of the festival.

The stadium, which has 15,000 seats, hosts some of the best bullfighters in the world. The festival features traditional bullfighting as well as bullfighters who ply their art from the back of highly trained horses.

Another Colombian festival that has been recognized by the United Nations is Pasto's Black and White Carnival, held after Christmas every year. The festival starts on December 28 with the Day of the Innocents, which is similar to April Fool's Day. There are street dances and concerts on January 5, El Día de los Negros (Day of the Blacks), and a huge parade on El Día de los Blancos (Day of the Whites) on January 6. The festival's origins can be traced to a slave rebellion in 1607.

Museums throughout Colombia introduce visitors to the history and culture of the various regions. At the Museo Etnográfico del Hombre Amazónico de Leticia on the Amazon River, visitors can learn about the ethnic groups of the Amazon.

Chapter

10

We Visit Colombia

As the level of violence in Colombia has gradually diminished, tourism has gradually increased. Colombia still does not receive the millions of visitors that go to Mexico or other popular tourist destinations, but travel to the country is growing. Colombians themselves are also being more adventurous about visiting unknown parts of their country. Let's take a look at some of the most exciting places to go in Colombia.

Starting at the very south of Colombia, the city of Leticia is on the Amazon River and right on the border with Brazil and Peru. Tour operators in Leticia will take visitors to see river dolphins, monkeys, and other Amazonian wildlife. Visitors who are reluctant to venture into the Amazon can see surprising clouds of small parrots flying all over the city square at dawn and dusk in downtown Leticia.

Popayán is one of Colombia's oldest cities. It is renowned throughout Colombia for its colonial architecture, red roofs, and white buildings. Popayán also has a national park, the Puracé, that includes caves, hot springs, grasslands, waterfalls, and a four-hour hiking trail to the peak of an inactive volcano.

Cali, Colombia's largest southern city, is the capital of the important sugar-growing department of Cauca. It is well known for its salsa and cumbia music, its famous Christmas festival, and its zoo, which is the best in the country. The large zoo hosts about 180 different species and is an important international research and conservation center.

Visitors to Colombia can see its beautiful coffee farms, where quaint farmhouses sit amid fields of small coffee bushes growing in the shade

The green iguana, which lives in the wild in Central and northern South America, can actually be a range of colors, from orange or pink to bright blue. It can grow to be 5 feet (1.5 meters) long. Popular as pets in the United States, green iguanas are farmed in Colombia and other South American countries.

of banana plants. The National Coffee Park near the town of Armenia combines attractions such as rides and go-karts with a museum, walking trails, and other ways to learn about coffee and Colombia. Visitors can stroll through an authentic farmhouse and also enjoy lunch at the park's excellent restaurants—with coffee, of course.

Another fantastic theme park is known as Piscilago (see pages 34–35), which is about two hours southwest of Bogotá in a town called Melgar. Piscilago is a water park and zoo that specializes in entertainment for the whole family.[1] It includes a waterslide that is about a quarter mile long—the longest in Latin America—and another mind-

Roller coaster at Colombian National Coffee Park

The main highway between San Gil (and Bogotá) and Bucaramanga winds down for about a mile (1.6 kilometers) through the Chicamocha Canyon.

blowing attraction in which visitors shoot down a super-fast slide and zoom around the inside of an enormous bowl until they drop through a hole into a deep pool of water below. Colsubsidio, one of Colombia's family benefit funds, owns Piscilago, so teachers and other workers who belong to the family benefit fund get discounts on admission.

Many of those workers live in Bogotá, a huge city that sits high in the eastern ridge of the Colombian Andes. The city lies along what is known as the Savannah of Bogotá, which is a surprisingly flat area of the Andes more than a mile and a half (2.4 kilometers) above sea level. Sometimes newcomers to the city need a day or two to get used to the altitude.

With a population of more than eight million people and numerous art galleries, shopping centers, museums, theaters, restaurants, and parks, there is plenty to do in Bogotá. Two highlights are the Gold Museum, which holds gold jewelry from throughout the history of

Colombia, and a special cable car that takes visitors up the steep slopes to the peak of Monserrate, a high ridge above the city.

Intrepid visitors can take another tourist train to the old salt-mining city of Zipaquirá, about 30 miles north of Bogotá. There, workers constructed a beautiful, large cathedral inside a salt mine.

The coast of Colombia offers more wonderful things to see and do. Cartagena is a living, breathing, museum, with huge thick walls built in the early days of the conquest. Tour guides are eager to usher visitors throughout the city in horse-drawn carriages. About an hour by boat from Cartagena lie the Islas Rosarios. The islands form a circle somewhat in the shape of a rosary necklace, thus the name, which is Spanish for "rosary." Visitors to the islands will be fascinated by the beaches, the aquarium, and the snorkeling.

The Salt Cathedral began as a small chapel where the miners would pray for blessings before beginning their work. It has been rebuilt and improved over the years and is now one of Colombia's most amazing buildings.

San Andrés Island is the largest island in the San Andrés Archipelago. Many of the residents are Afro-Colombian and speak a form of English.

More beaches and snorkeling are available at the San Andrés Archipelago, which belongs to Colombia, although it is 500 miles (800 kilometers) northwest of the mainland—much closer to Nicaragua than Colombia. The islands have a long and colorful history, including legends of buried treasure and arguments about whether they really belong to Colombia.

The descendents of African slaves who were brought to the islands in the 1600s still live there, and speak their own unique language that is a mix of English and African languages. The United Nations Educational, Scientific and Cultural Organization has named San Andrés a marine biosphere preserve because of the extensive coral reefs and mangrove swamps.

Rice Pudding

Rice pudding is so popular in Colombia that sometimes Colombians don't even wait to chill it. They might make rice pudding in the morning and eat it for breakfast, but it is mainly a popular dessert.

Ingredients
¼ cup rice
2 cups milk
2 egg yolks
¼ cup sugar
¼ teaspoon salt
1 teaspoon vanilla
Optional: Top with cinnamon, whipped cream and a maraschino cherry

Directions
1. With the help of an adult, boil water in the bottom of a double boiler, and then lower the heat to medium.
2. Place the milk and rice in the top of the double boiler and cook for 45 to 50 minutes, stirring occasionally, until the rice is soft and has absorbed much of the milk.
3. In a small bowl, mix the egg yolks and the sugar.
4. Stir two tablespoons of the rice and milk mixture into the egg yolks and sugar mixture.
5. Add the new mixture to the top of the double boiler and cook for five more minutes, stirring constantly.
6. Remove from heat and add the vanilla.
7. Place in a serving dish and chill. Serve plain or decorated with cinnamon, whipped cream, and a maraschino cherry.

Colombian-style Appliqué

Colombian primitive appliqué is popular in Colombia. It is used in wall hangings and to decorate clothes and handbags. Here are the materials and directions for an appliqué hat.

Materials
1 plain white hat (from craft store)
felt in various colors
scissors
glue
fabric paint

Directions
1. Choose a pastoral setting you would like to present, such as a hillside or a farm.
2. Cut out shapes to represent the animals or the people.
3. Glue the shapes to the hat.
4. Use paint for grass and trees.

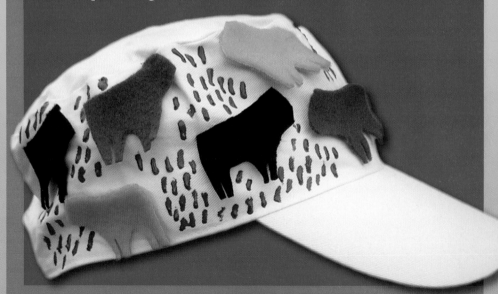

CHAPTER NOTES

Chapter 1. Welcome to Colombia
1. "The Nobel Prize in Literature 1982: Gabriel García Márquez," http://nobelprize.org/nobel_prizes/literature/laureates/1982/
2. "Colombia Official Tourism Portal," http://www.turismocolombia.com/en/

Chapter 2. A Brief History of Colombia
1. Simon Romero. "Manuel Marulanda, Top Commander of Colombia's Largest Guerrilla Group, Is Dead," *The New York Times*, May 26, 2008, http://www.nytimes.com/2008/05/26/world/americas/26marulanda.html?fta=y

Chapter 3. The Land
1. Victoria Bruce, *No Apparent Danger: The True Story of Volcanic Disaster at Galeras and Nevado del Ruiz* (New York: HarperCollins, 2001), p. 222.

Chapter 5. Culture and Lifestyle
1. Angus Deaton, Ph.D., "Income, Health, and Well-Being Around the World: Evidence From the Gallup World Poll." Reprinted with permission from *Journal of Economic Perspectives*, Volume 22, Number 2, Spring 2008 (http://www.aeaweb.org/jep), http://media.gallup.com/dataviz/www/Angus_Deaton_Gallup_Poll_Article.pdf

Chapter 7. Politics and Government
1. Marc Gonsalves, Keith Stansell, Tom Howes, and Gary Brozek, *Out of Captivity: Surviving 1,967 Days in the Colombian Jungle* (New York: HarperCollins, 2009), p. 423.

Chapter 8. Famous People
1. Roberta Smith, "Botero Restores the Dignity of Prisoners at Abu Ghraib," *The New York Times*, November 15, 2006, http://www.nytimes.com/2006/11/15/arts/design/15chan.html
2. Carlos Valderrama, *MLSNet.com*, http://www.mlssoccer.com/player/carlos-valderrama

Chapter 10. We Visit Colombia
1. Rebecca Thatcher Murcia, "For the Public Good," *Funworld*, October 2009, p. 56, http://www.iaapa.org/industry/funworld/2009/oct/features/Piscilago/index.asp

BCE

10,000   Indigenous societies develop complex organizations and trade with one another throughout what is present-day Colombia.

1500 CE   Explorers from Europe first arrive.

1510   San Sebastian is settled in Urabá, but does not last.

1526   Santa Marta, the oldest continually existing city in Colombia, is founded.

1538   Gonzalo Jiménez de Quesada founds Bogotá.

1621   Benkos Biohó, who escaped from slavery and founded a freed slave community near Cartagena called San Basilio de Palenque, is executed by the Spanish authorities.

1749   The viceroyalty of New Granada is founded with Bogotá as the capital.

1810   The period Colombian historians refer to as the Foolish Fatherland begins, with colonists fighting between themselves.

1819   Rebellious colonialists win independence from Spain. Gran Colombia is formed.

1830   Gran Colombia is dissolved. Simón Bolívar, who led the fight for independence from Spain, dies.

1839   Civil war between conservatives and liberals begins and lasts three years.

1869   A leprosy epidemic begins in Colombia.

1899   The War of a Thousand Days lasts until 1902.

1903   With U.S. backing, Panama secedes from Colombia.

1928   The banana workers strike; soldiers kill about 73 people.

1948   Presidential candidate Jorge Eliécer Gaitán is assassinated; violence breaks out.

1954   The legislature approves a law creating family benefit funds for all Colombian workers.

1964   The FARC is founded by Manuel Marulanda and Jacobo Arenas.

1985   M-19 guerrillas take over the Palace of Justice; the military invades and 55 people die.

1987   Jaime Pardo Leal, the presidential candidate of the legal wing of the FARC, the Patriotic Union, is assassinated; the Patriotic Union eventually dissolves.

1989   Luis Carlos Galán, a presidential candidate, is assassinated.

1991   Colombia approves a more democratic constitution.

2002   Presidential candidate Ingrid Betancourt is kidnapped by the FARC. Álvaro Uribe is elected.

2003   Guillermo Gaviria, a Colombian politician who led a march against violence, dies a year after being kidnapped by the FARC.

2006   Uribe is reelected.

2008   Manuel Marulanda, the founder of the FARC, dies.

2009   Three U.S. military contractors—Marc Gonsalves, Keith Stansell, and Tom Howes—publish the bestseller *Out of Captivity: Surviving 1,967 Days in the Colombian Jungle.*

2010   Although liberal candidates attract many supporters, Álvaro Uribe's defense minister, Juan Manuel Santos, emerges as the winner after two rounds of voting for the new president.

Books

Bloom, Harold. *Gabriel García Márquez* (Bloom's BioCritiques). Broomall, PA: Chelsea House Publishers, 2006.

Diego, Ximena. *Shakira: Woman Full of Grace.* New York: Fireside, 2001.

Mulder, Michelle. *Yeny and the Children for Peace.* Toronto: Second Story Press, 2008.

Rice, Earle, Jr. *A Brief Political and Geographic History of Latin America: Where Are Gran Colombia, La Plata, and Dutch Guiana?* Hockessin, DE: Mitchell Lane Publishers, 2008.

Smith, Roberta. "Botero Restores the Dignity of Prisoners at Abu Ghraib," *The New York Times,* November 15, 2006. http://www.nytimes.com/2006/11/15/arts/design/15chan.html

Woods, Sara. *Colombia.* Guilford, CT: Globe Pequot Press, 2008.

Works Consulted

Betancourt, Ingrid. *Until Death Do Us Part.* New York: HarperCollins, 2008.

Bruce, Victoria. *No Apparent Danger: The True Story of Volcanic Disaster at Galeras and Nevado del Ruiz.* New York: Harper Collins, 2001.

Bushnell, David. *Una Nación a Pesar de Si Misma.* Bogotá: Planeta, 2007.

"Condena al Reclutador de 'Falsos Positivos.' " *ElTiempo.com,* October 2, 2009.

Deaton, Angus, Ph.D. "Income, Health, and Well-Being Around the World: Evidence From the Gallup World Poll." Reprinted with permission from *Journal of Economic Perspectives,* Volume 22, Number 2, Spring 2008 (http://www.aeaweb.org/jep). http://media.gallup.com/dataviz/www/Angus_Deaton_Gallup_Poll_Article.pdf

Dudley, Steven. *Walking Ghosts: Murder and Guerrilla Politics in Colombia.* New York: Routledge, 2004.

Faerna, Jose Maria. *Botero.* New York: Harry N. Abrams, 1997.

Gonsalves, Marc, Keith Stansell, Tom Howes, and Gary Brozek. *Out of Captivity: Surviving 1,967 Days in the Colombian Jungle.* New York: HarperCollins, 2009.

Kirk, Robin. *More Terrible Than Death: Drugs, Violence and America's War in Colombia.* New York: Public Affairs, 2004.

MLSNet.Com, http://www.mlssoccer.com/player/carlos-valderrama

Romero, Simon. "Manuel Marulanda, Top Commander of Colombia's Largest Guerrilla Group, Is Dead," *The New York Times,* May 26, 2008, http://www.nytimes.com/2008/05/26/world/americas/26marulanda.html?fta=y

Weisman, Alan. *Gaviotas: A Village to Reinvent the World.* White River Junction, VT: Chelsea Green Publishing Company, 1998.

On the Internet

Barefoot Foundation
  http://www.barefootfoundation.com

CIA World Factbook: Colombia
  https://www.cia.gov/library/publications/the-world-factbook/geos/co.html

Colombia: Official Tourism Website
  http://www.colombiaespasion.com

Colombia Travel
  http://www.colombia.travel/en/

U.S. Department of State: Colombia
  http://www.state.gov/r/pa/ei/bgn/35754.htm

archipelago (ar-kuh-PEH-luh-goh)—A chain of islands.

Centrist (SEN-trist)—A person who holds moderate political views.

communion (kuh-MYOON-yun)—The acting of consuming the Eucharist to commemorate the death of Jesus.

democratic (deh-moh-KRAA-tic)—Using equal participation in the making of decisions.

Eucharist (YOO-kar-ist)—The bread and the wine that Christians eat at communion to commemorate the death of Jesus.

Federalist (FEH-duh-ruh-list)—A supporter of the federal system of government, which gives power to state governments.

guerrilla (guh-RIH-luh)—An irregular armed group that attempts to overthrow an established government.

hooliganism (HOO-luh-gan-ism)—Acts of vandalism peformed by groups, usually sports fans.

humanitarian (hyoo-mah-nih-TAYR-ee-an)—Caring for the lives of other people.

immunity (ih-MYOO-nih-tee)—The body's ability to resist an illness.

indigenous (in-DIH-jih-nus)—Native or original to a region.

paramilitary (payr-uh-MIL-ih-tayr-ee)—Armed groups that imitate the military but are not actually military.

populist (POP-yoo-list)—A political belief that advocates the interests of ordinary men and women.

rosary (ROH-sah-ree)—A string of beads used by Catholics for prayers.

sacrament (SAK-rah-ment)—Something considered to be sacred.

socialist (SOH-shuh-list)—A political system that distributes goods and services based on fairness and equity rather than the traditional market.

secession (suh-SEH-shun)—The political break of part of a country into its own country.

PHOTO CREDITS: Cover, pp. 1, 10–11, 26, 45, 47, 53—cc-by-nc-sa-2.0; pp. 2–3, 4–5, 27, 32, 38–39, 46, 52, 54, 55, 56—cc-by-nc-nd-sa-2.0; pp. 14, 42, 43, 44, 45, 50—cc-by-sa-2.0; p. 17—cc-by-sa-2.5; p. 19—AFP; p. 21—NASA; cc-by-sa-3.0; pp. 23, 28, 34–35, 57, 58—Rebecca Thatcher Murcia; pp. 30, 31, 48—David Rich. Every effort has been made to locate all copyright holders of material used in this book. If any errors or omissions have occurred, corrections will be made in future editions of the book.

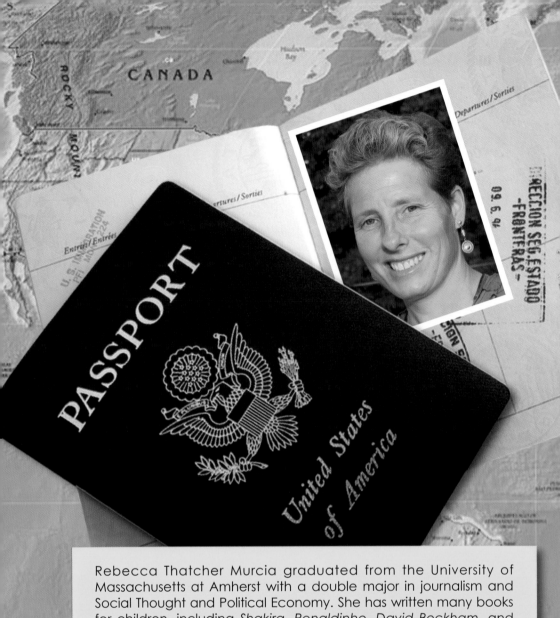

Rebecca Thatcher Murcia graduated from the University of Massachusetts at Amherst with a double major in journalism and Social Thought and Political Economy. She has written many books for children, including *Shakira, Ronaldinho, David Beckham,* and *Meet Our New Student from Colombia* for Mitchell Lane Publishers. Her husband, Saúl Murcia, grew up in Colombia. After he died of cancer in 2005, Rebecca and her two sons, Gabriel and Mario, and their dog, Crystal, moved to La Mesa, a small town in Colombia. Gabriel and Mario enrolled in school in La Mesa, and also played for the town's soccer and tennis teams. During their vacation, they explored Colombia's Caribbean coast, snorkeling in Las Islas Rosarios and playing in the waves in Cartagena. Find out more about Rebecca at http://www.thatchermurcia.com.